Praise for
Your Health and Medical Workbook
by Dylan Landis

"The key to accurate diagnosis and treatment is very often a complete medical history. Unfortunately, details of past illnesses and medical care are often incomplete or lost. Dylan Landis's *Your Health and Medical Workbook* provides a simple but elegant method of maintaining complete medical records at home—records that may very well help ensure your good care in the future."

> —Robert A. Meyers, M.D., Associate Attending Physician of Medicine and Pulmonary Diseases, St. Luke's/Roosevelt Hospital Center, New York City

"Accurate historic information remains the cornerstone of good health care despite a world of sophisticated medical technology. This is never more important than at a time of illness when it is often least accessible. Memory may be insufficient to recall this information.

"Utilizing this outline by Dylan Landis, the layperson can learn to record health information that may prove invaluable in the future. By faithfully doing this, the patient enters into a constructive partnership with those responsible for delivering health care. **I strongly recommend reading and following the suggestions outlined in this book.**"

> —Howard Goldin, M.C., Clinical Professor of Medicine and Attending Physician, The New York Hospital–Cornell Medical Center, and Consulting Physician to the Hospital of Rockefeller University

NOW YOU CAN KEEP TRACK OF . . .

- YOUR DOCTOR APPOINTMENTS
- NAMES OF SPECIALISTS
- RECURRING PROBLEMS, LIKE HEADACHES
- YOUR FAMILY'S MEDICAL HISTORY
- AND MUCH MORE

. . . ALL IN ONE PLACE—with . . .

Your Health and Medical Workbook

YOUR HEALTH AND MEDICAL WORKBOOK

DYLAN LANDIS

BERKLEY BOOKS, NEW YORK

YOUR HEALTH AND MEDICAL WORKBOOK

A Berkley Book / published by arrangement with
the author

PRINTING HISTORY
Berkley trade paperback edition / February 1995

ISBN: 0-425-15839-X

BERKLEY®
Berkley Books are published by The Berkley Publishing Group,
200 Madison Avenue, New York, New York 10016.
BERKLEY and the "B" design
are trademarks belonging to Berkley Publishing Corporation.

PRINTED IN THE UNITED STATES OF AMERICA

10 9 8 7 6 5 4 3 2 1

This book contains personal medical information. If you find it, please return it to:

Name _____

Address _____

_____

_____

_____

Telephone _____

Contents

Contents

ACKNOWLEDGMENTS

Many thanks to the physicians who contributed ideas to this workbook, particularly Dr. Thomas L. Leaman, Professor Emeritus of Family and Community Medicine at Penn State College of Medicine; and Dr. J. Christopher Shank, Chairman, Department of Family Practice at Fairview General Hospital, Cleveland. Both are former chairmen of the medical records committee of the Society of Teachers of Family Medicine. I am also grateful to Dr. Larry L. Dickey, a faculty member of the Department of Family and Community Medicine at the University of California in San Francisco, who shared his own research on record-keeping by patients.

Thanks also to Rachael Cronin at Milcom, a division of Hollister, Inc., for sharing the record-keeping forms they supply to doctors. Roger Sherwood, executive director of the Society of Teachers of Family Medicine, the organization that helped develop the Milcom forms, suggested several excellent sources of information. Michael Copeland at the American Academy of Pediatrics and Joann Schellenbach at the American Cancer Society were also generous with their time and explanations.

Finally, thanks to Elaine Breiger and Dorothy Greene, who showed me the value of keeping good medical notes; to Erica Landis, who came up with the idea for a comprehensive workbook; to Dr. Bern Landis, whose suggestions appear throughout these pages; to Dominick Abel, my agent; and to Elizabeth Beier, my editor.

YOUR HEALTH AND MEDICAL WORKBOOK

HOW TO USE THIS BOOK

When my aunt Dorothy was hospitalized a few years ago, she discovered that getting sick is not just alarming, it is confusing. Medications are prescribed, dosages get altered, then new drugs are added to the mix. Tests are taken, the results assessed, and more tests scheduled. In the hospital, residents sometimes ask *you* to recite the litany of your tests and medications. Being sick entails a whirlwind of data, and as Dorothy realized, one person has the strongest motivation for keeping track of it all: the patient.

My aunt's sister made her a medical diary. It was a chronological list of her doctor's appointments, tests, changes in medication, even questions she wanted to remember to ask. If a drug had side effects, we wrote them down. If lowering the dosage helped, we asked the new dosage and wrote that down, too.

Some doctors not only looked at her chart, they started reading the diary. "Who put this together?" one specialist asked, intrigued, then sat down and read every page. When he was finished, it was obvious he had a clearer long-range picture of her condition, as if the fragments of a puzzle had coalesced. More importantly, through her own grasp of the information, Dorothy became a partner in her treatment, not just a passive receiver of care.

You don't need a medical emergency to make record-keeping worthwhile. Just the sight of a white coat can be stressful enough to literally raise your blood pressure, making you forget those pressing questions you wanted to ask (at least until you're halfway home). If you can't recall details of your past medical care, a new doctor may be at a disadvantage. Can you remember the year of your last tetanus shot? Which antibiotic upsets your stomach? If your child is sick, can you tell the pediatrician how high his fever was three days ago, two days ago, yesterday? Not unless you've been writing it down.

Indeed, most doctors who learned I was writing this workbook had one thing to say: "That's the kind of thing I'd love to photocopy if a patient filled it out."

Nine Great Reasons to Write Your Own Medical History

You'll have all the facts at your fingertips. If you see more than one doctor or periodically change physicians, you'll be asked each time for an accurate, detailed medical history. Having all the answers in one place is a big help, both to you and the doctor.

You might get more money back. Track bills and insurance payments on the pages provided to make sure you get every reimbursement and tax deduction you're owed.

You might stay healthier. The workbook actually prompts you with medically recommended schedules of tests, vaccinations, and checkups to keep your health care up-to-date. Your own entries are reminders, too, to phone or visit the doctor for a follow-up.

You won't feel helpless when you're sick. This workbook can give you a clear picture of any health problems and medical care, not just now but over time. It can also enhance communication with your doctor. Those two critical factors give you a far greater sense of empowerment.

You'll know what questions to ask. Write them down as they occur to you before each doctor's appointment, bring the book with you, and note the answers. Now they're permanently on file for your review.

You'll make better decisions. When all the information is written down, it's easier to sort through any differences in doctors' recommendations, factor in second opinions, and weigh your medical options.

You can give a child a great start. Any time from birth on, start in the pediatric chapter and create a written record of your child's health care. It's a legacy he can add to—and refer to—throughout life.

You'll learn what runs in the family. Most people have no idea of their grandparents' illnesses or causes of death. By filling out a personal family history, you might uncover patterns or genetic tendencies, and that's a first step toward good preventive medicine.

You can track your progress if you're sick. The workbook includes a diary of your doctor's visits, and pages to record any treatments, medications, surgeries, hospitalizations, and their results.

In the end, you're not trying to become a medical expert—that's your doctor's role—but an informed and responsible patient.

How the book works

This book is easy to use. Just fill in the blanks. If you want to elaborate, add your own notes. If a question doesn't apply, leave it blank or write NA (not applicable).

You might want to photocopy the forms you use most—for example, the Diary of Doctors' Appointments and the Medication Log. When the workbook is full, you can start using these copies and keep them in your personal files.

How to keep this workbook for a child

Begin with the last two chapters. One is for your child's background health information, the other is a record of visits to the pediatrician.

Use the other chapters, too, to record your child's emergency information, medications, doctors' names and numbers, insurance data, and so on.

Do you have to answer every question in the workbook?

Absolutely not. It's worth doing a little research and asking relatives a few questions to make the workbook as complete a resource as possible, but these personal records are designed to be an aid, not a challenge.

Where do you start?

Start wherever it's easy and satisfying to dig in.

Try filling out the Address Book, a simple list (and fast resource) of your health care providers. If you're seeing a doctor soon, start with the Diary of Doctors' Appointments.

If you're beginning this workbook for a child, bring it along when you next see the pediatrician; she or a nurse can easily check your child's chart for the information you want. If the records don't go back to birth, call or write your obstetrician with a list of specific questions.

May this workbook see you through years of good health—and good health care.

Emergency Information and Fast Reference

Keep a photocopy of this worksheet in your wallet.

Name _____ Social Security no. _____

Address _____

Telephone (day)_____ (home) _____

Date of birth _____ Driver's lic. no. _____

Required daily medications and dosage _____

Other medications now being taken (use pencil) _____

Allergies (foods, medications, etc.) _____

Medical conditions _____

Blood type _____ Past surgeries _____

Are you hearing impaired? ☐ yes ☐ no

Wear a hearing aid? ☐ yes ☐ no   Use sign language?
    ☐ yes ☐ no

Do you wear contact lenses? ☐ yes ☐ no

Do you wear removable bridges? ☐ yes ☐ no

Are you diabetic? ☐ yes ☐ no   Epileptic? ☐ yes ☐ no

Do you wear a pacemaker? ☐ yes ☐ no

    Type, make, model _____

Are you a U.S. Veteran? ☐ yes ☐ no

Emergency phone numbers

People to contact in an emergency:

Name _____

Relationship _____

Telephone number _____

Name _____

Relationship _____

Telephone number _____

Insurance company _____

Policy number _____

Group number _____

Telephone _____

Preauthorization needed for hospitalization? ☐ yes   ☐ no

Telephone for preauthorization _____

Have you signed any of the following forms?
    ☐ living will   ☐ organ donor*
    ☐ power of attorney for health care   ☐ health care proxy form

Where are these documents filed? _____

_____

*For information on organ donation, call the Living Bank and Registry at (800) 528-2971.

Address Book:
Health Care Providers

Emergency Phone Numbers

Ambulance _____

Police _____

Poison Control_____ (*A state hot line, this number is probably listed in the front of your telephone directory.*)

Hospital emergency room _____

Other emergency numbers _____

Other hot lines _____

Primary Care

My primary physician _____

Address _____

Telephone _____

Notes _____

Pediatrician _____

Address _____

Telephone _____

Notes _____

Pharmacies

Local pharmacy _____
Hours _____
Address _____
Telephone _____
Notes _____

24-hour pharmacy _____
Address _____
Telephone _____
Notes _____

Pharmacy that delivers _____
Hours _____
Address _____
Telephone _____
Notes _____
_____
_____
_____

Other Health Care Providers

Dentist _____
Address _____
Telephone _____
Notes _____

Oral surgeon _____
Address _____
Telephone _____
Notes _____

Ophthalmologist _____
Address _____
Telephone _____
Notes _____

Eyeglass store/optometrist _____
Address _____
Telephone _____
　　　My eyeglass Rx _____
Notes _____

Psychotherapist _____
Address _____
Telephone _____
Notes _____

Specialists

Specialty _____
Name _____
Address _____
Telephone _____
Notes _____

Specialty _____
Name _____
Address _____
Telephone _____
Notes _____

Specialty _____
Name _____
Address _____
Telephone _____
Notes _____

Specialty _____
Name _____
Address _____
Telephone _____
Notes _____

Specialty _____
Name _____
Address _____
Telephone _____
Notes _____

Specialty _____
Name _____
Address _____
Telephone _____
Notes _____

Specialty _____
Name _____
Address _____
Telephone _____
Notes _____

Specialty _____
Name _____
Address _____
Telephone _____
Notes _____

Specialty _____
Name _____
Address _____
Telephone _____
Notes _____

Specialty _____
Name _____
Address _____
Telephone _____
Notes _____

Specialty _____
Name _____
Address _____
Telephone _____
Notes _____

Support Groups

Group _____
Meeting times _____
Address _____
Telephone _____
Notes _____
_____
_____
_____
_____

Group _____
Meeting times _____
Address _____
Telephone _____
Notes _____
_____
_____
_____
_____

Group _____
Meeting times _____
Address _____
Telephone _____
Notes _____
_____
_____
_____
_____

My Former Health Care Providers

List any health professionals you no longer see but who may have your old medical records on file.

Name and specialty _____

Address _____

Telephone _____

Notes _____

_____

_____

_____

Name and specialty _____

Address _____

Telephone _____

Notes _____

_____

_____

_____

Name and specialty _____

Address _____

Telephone _____

Notes _____

_____

_____

_____

Insurance Information

In an emergency or for hospital admissions, you may need this information fast. If you use an HMO or Medicare, skip the questions on insurance companies.

Primary Insurance

Company _____

Type of coverage: ☐ Family ☐ Individual

Name of insured _____

Social Security no. _____

Policy no. _____ Group no. _____

Also covers: ☐ dental ☐ vision ☐ psychotherapy

Deductible _____ Copayment _____

Out-of-pocket maximum _____

Maximum lifetime coverage _____

Need second opinion for surgery? ☐ yes ☐ no

Telephone no. to call for approval for hospitalization or outpatient procedures _____

Call within _____ hours for emergency admittance authorization

Telephone no. for general information _____

Cost of policy _____

Where my insurance forms & data are filed _____

Dental Insurance

Company _____

Address _____

Telephone _____ Policy no. _____

Write the name of your insurance-approved dentist in the Address Book, page 13.

Optical Insurance

Company _____

Address _____

Telephone _____ Policy no. _____

Write the name of your insurance-approved eye doctors in the Address Book, page 13.

Prescription Medication Insurance

Mail-order source, if any _____

Company _____

Address _____

Telephone _____ Policy or I.D. no. _____

Write the name of your insurance-approved pharmacies in the Address Book, page 13.

Secondary Insurance

Company _____

Type of coverage: ☐ Family ☐ Individual

Name of insured _____

Social Security no. _____

Policy no. _____ Group no. _____

Also covers: ☐ dental ☐ vision ☐ psychotherapy

Deductible _____ Copayment _____

Out-of-pocket maximum _____

Maximum lifetime coverage _____

Need second opinion for surgery? ☐ yes ☐ no

Telephone no. to call for approval for hospitalization or outpatient procedures _____

    Call within _____ hours for emergency admittance authorization

Telephone no. for general information _____

Cost of policy _____

Where my insurance forms & data are filed _____

HMO Information

HMO name _____

Member services telephone no. _____

Member I.D. (or Social Security) no. _____

My primary HMO physician _____

Medical center name _____

Address _____

Telephone no. _____

Days & hours open _____

Notes _____

Copayments? (describe, if any) _____

Dental coverage? ☐ yes ☐ no

Optical coverage? ☐ yes ☐ no

    Pharmacy approved by HMO _____

    Address _____

    Telephone no. _____

    Hours _____

    Delivery? ☐ yes ☐ no

Telephone no. to call for emergency medical treatment _____

    Call within _____ hours for emergency doctor's appointment

    Call within _____ hours for emergency hospitalization

Where my HMO forms and data are filed _____

Medicare Information

Medicare number _____

Local Medicare office _____

_____

Telephone _____

Notes _____

Disability and Life Insurance

DISABILITY INSURANCE

Company _____

Address _____

Telephone _____ Policy no. _____

LIFE INSURANCE

Company _____

Address _____

Telephone _____ Policy no. _____

MY INSURANCE AGENT

Name _____

Company _____

Address _____

Telephone _____

MEDICATION LOG

Use this section to track all the medications you take, including over-the-counter drugs.

The worksheet for prescription drugs asks detailed questions, which can be helpful if you take several drugs at once or periodically change medications. Otherwise, just fill out the parts that seem most useful.

Remember to ask your doctor about any drug she prescribes: Are there side effects? Interactions with foods, alcohol, or other types of medications? Should this medication be taken with food or water? Your pharmacist can also give you information on any prescription drug.

Over-the-Counter Remedies Used

Brand _____ How often _____

Brand _____ How often _____

Brand _____ How often _____

Brand _____ How often _____

Notes _____

_____

RECORD OF PRESCRIPTION DRUGS

Date	Medica-tion	Generic name, if used	Name of prescrib-ing doctor	Why prescribed	Dosage: amount, how often, how long	Results
23/08 94	Lomotil		Pungur	I.B.S.		does not prevent attacks
	HRT Premarin .625		Pungur	HRT	.625 mg	
	Prometrium		Pungur	HRT	100 mg.	
	Modulon		Pungur	I.BS motility regulator		does not prevent attacks
	Buscopan		Pungur	IBS antispasmodic		good -after attack
12/09 97	Topicort		Pungur	eczema		effective
26/05 99	Anti vert		Pungur	vertigo		

Special instructions	Side effects	Pharmacy name and telephone	Rx number	No. of refills	Dates refilled
			207 5039	none	
Taken until Sept 2002 June 06 01					
Taken until Sept 2002 June 6/01					

RECORD OF PRESCRIPTION DRUGS

Date	Medica-tion	Generic name, if used	Name of prescrib-ing doctor	Why prescribed	Dosage: amount, how often, how long	Results
26/05 99	SERC		Pungur	Vertigo		
29/05 99	Viaderm		Pungur	Canker sores	as needed 3 times/ day	good
99-2000	Lipitor		Pungur	Cholesterol		
Jan 18 2000	Dicetel 50mg		Tedorak	IBS	3 time per day as needed	very good.
Feb 17 2000	Apo diazepam 5mg.		Kostiuk	TMJ	½ tablet (100 tabs)	
June 8 2000	Cotridin Syrup		DeWitt medicentre	Cough		
Oct 99	Didrocal		Pungur	Osteoporosis		Lost 3.7% bone density

Special instructions	Side effects	Pharmacy name and telephone	Rx number	No. of refills	Dates refilled
			6197693		no refills
	Sun sensetivity				
max dosage 6 tablets per day.	drowsiness		0036 2758 6012180		
			6012210		
Last prescription filled 08/01 for 6 months			↓		taken for 1 year

Medication Log

RECORD OF PRESCRIPTION DRUGS

Date	Medica-tion	Generic name, if used	Name of prescrib-ing doctor	Why prescribed	Dosage: amount, how often, how long	Results
Sept 15 2000	Diclofenac 5% Gel		Pungur	Osteo Arthritis Pain		
Oct 16 2000	Losec 20 mg		Pungur	Stomach Acid	15 tabs.	
Oct 12 2000	Tylenol 3		Pator medicentre	headaches	20 tabs	
June 25 2001	Fem HRT		Pungur		28 tabs.	Bleeding Biopsy
July 20 2001	Celebrex 200mg.		Pungur	Osteoarthritis	40 caps	
July 20 2001	Premarin					
	Prometrium					

Special instructions	Side effects	Pharmacy name and telephone	Rx number	No. of refills	Dates refilled
			603 5073		
			603 1600		
			203 9144		
			606 9940		
			607 3125		
			607 3126		
			607 3127		

MEDICAL HISTORY

This section contains a detailed personal and family history and a record of your exposure to any environmental hazards. The history is particularly helpful when you see a doctor for the first time. It can also reveal any patterns of illness that may run in your family, and which might bear watching or preventive treatment.

Check under *Self* if you've ever had any of the following conditions. For relatives, note the name and family relationship (sister, first cousin) under *Family*. Be sure to record details about any conditions, their treatment, and outcome at the end under *Details and Explanations*.

Conditions

Condition	Self	Family
Alcoholism	☐	_____
Allergies	☐	_____
Anemia	☐	_____
Arthritis or joint problems	☐	_____
Asthma	☐	_____

Condition	Self	Family	Medical History
Back problems	☐	_____	
Bowel problems (colitis, constipation, etc.)	☐	_____	
Breathing disorders (emphysema, bronchitis, etc.)	☐	_____	
Cancer or tumors	☐	_____	
Cough, persistent	☐	_____	
Cystic fibrosis	☐	_____	
Depression	☐	_____	
DES exposure during mother's pregnancy	☐	_____	
Diabetes	☐	_____	
Drug abuse	☐	_____	
Eating disorders	☐	_____	
Epilepsy or seizures	☐	_____	
Exposure to chemicals or toxic substances	☐	_____	
Eye problems or glaucoma	☐	_____	
Gastrointestinal or stomach problems	☐	_____	
Genetic conditions	☐	_____	
Gynecological conditions	☐	_____	
Headache or migraine	☐	_____	
Hearing defects	☐	_____	
Heart conditions	☐	_____	
Hemorrhoids or other rectal problems	☐	_____	
Hepatitis or other liver disease	☐	_____	
Hernia or rupture	☐	_____	
High blood pressure	☐	_____	
Kidney or bladder problems	☐	_____	
Mental retardation	☐	_____	
Mononucleosis	☐	_____	
Mumps, measles, or chicken pox	☐	_____	
Neuralgia or neuritis	☐	_____	
Obesity	☐	_____	
Pap smear irregularities	☐	_____	
Phlebitis	☐	_____	
Premenstrual syndrome	☐	_____	

Condition	Self	Family
Psychological conditions	☐	_____
Rheumatic fever	☐	_____
Rubella (German measles)	☐	_____
Scarlet fever	☐	_____
Sexually transmitted diseases	☐	_____
Skin problems	☐	_____
Sleep problems	☐	_____
Stress, tension, or anxiety	☐	_____
Stroke	☐	_____
Suicide or suicide attempt	☐	_____
Thyroid disease	☐	_____
Ulcer	☐	_____
Other_____	☐	_____
Other_____	☐	_____

Family Background

List your relatives' race and ethnic or national background:

Mother _____ Father _____

Mother's parents _____

Father's parents _____

Causes of Death

Record the cause and age at death for close relatives (grandparents, parents, siblings, children, aunts, and uncles).

Maternal grandmother _____ Age _____

Maternal grandfather _____ Age _____

Paternal grandmother _____ Age _____

Paternal grandfather _____ Age _____

Mother _____ Age _____

Father _____ Age _____

Other relatives _____ Age _____

_____ Age _____

_____ Age _____

Environmental Exposures

If you have ever been exposed to potential or known hazards for more than a brief period, record it here. Include anything you can think of. A few examples: all kinds of dusts (coal, asbestos, manufacturing, etc.), fumes, gases, chemicals (such as insecticides or paint), cigarette smoke (your own or someone else's), radiation, long-term loud noises.

First list the types of jobs you have held; it may cue your doctor in to exposures you weren't aware of.

Job   Your age at time

_____   _____
_____   _____
_____   _____
_____   _____
_____   _____
_____   _____

Type of exposure _____

How long _____ When _____

Where _____

Protective measures used _____

Reactions at time of exposure _____

Notes _____

Type of exposure _____

How long _____ When _____

Where _____

Protective measures used _____

Reactions at time of exposure _____

Notes _____

Details and Explanations

_____
_____
_____
_____
_____
_____
_____
_____
_____
_____
_____
_____
_____
_____
_____
_____
_____
_____
_____
_____
_____
_____
_____
_____
_____
_____
_____
_____

Diary of doctors' Appointments

There's nothing like a written record of office visits to give you a long-term overview of your own health. Taking notes also preserves the details of a conversation, making it easier to follow a doctor's instructions or compare different opinions.

Write down questions *before* an appointment, so nothing important goes unasked. (Use that section of each entry for the answers, too.)

Do you have to record every routine visit? Not necessarily, but it might help you spot patterns in minor complaints and let you compare treatments over time. If you're running out of entries, try photocopying a blank one, and keep the copies in your own files.

Diary of Doctors' Appointments

Reason for visit _____

Date _____   Doctor _____

Describe problem, if any _____

Cause of problem _____

Doctor's advice and treatment _____

_____

_____

Tests performed, if any _____

Test results _____

Recommended follow-up _____

_____

Questions to ask during this visit _____

_____

_____

_____

_____

_____

_____

Doctor's answers and comments _____

_____

_____

_____

_____

_____

Reason for visit _____

Date _____   Doctor _____

Describe problem, if any _____

Cause of problem _____

Doctor's advice and treatment _____

_____

_____

Tests performed, if any _____

Test results _____

Recommended follow-up _____

_____

Questions to ask during this visit _____

_____

_____

_____

_____

_____

_____

Doctor's answers and comments _____

_____

_____

_____

_____

33

Diary of Doctors' Appointments

Reason for visit _____

Date _____   Doctor _____

Describe problem, if any _____

Cause of problem _____

Doctor's advice and treatment _____

_____

_____

Tests performed, if any _____

Test results _____

Recommended follow-up _____

_____

Questions to ask during this visit _____

_____

_____

_____

_____

_____

Doctor's answers and comments _____

_____

_____

_____

_____

Reason for visit _____

Date _____   Doctor _____

Describe problem, if any _____

Cause of problem _____

Doctor's advice and treatment _____

_____

_____

Tests performed, if any _____

Test results _____

Recommended follow-up _____

_____

Questions to ask during this visit _____

_____

_____

_____

_____

_____

Doctor's answers and comments _____

_____

_____

_____

_____

Diary of Doctors' Appointments

Reason for visit _____

Date _____   Doctor _____

Describe problem, if any _____

Cause of problem _____

Doctor's advice and treatment _____

_____

_____

Tests performed, if any _____

Test results _____

Recommended follow-up _____

_____

Questions to ask during this visit _____

_____

_____

_____

_____

_____

_____

Doctor's answers and comments _____

_____

_____

_____

_____

Reason for visit _____

Date _____   Doctor _____

Describe problem, if any _____

Cause of problem _____

Doctor's advice and treatment _____

_____

_____

Tests performed, if any _____

Test results _____

Recommended follow-up _____

_____

Questions to ask during this visit _____

_____

_____

_____

_____

_____

Doctor's answers and comments _____

_____

_____

_____

_____

Diary of Doctors' Appointments

Reason for visit _____

Date _____ Doctor _____

Describe problem, if any _____

Cause of problem _____

Doctor's advice and treatment _____

_____

_____

Tests performed, if any _____

Test results _____

Recommended follow-up _____

_____

Questions to ask during this visit _____

_____

_____

_____

_____

_____

Doctor's answers and comments _____

_____

_____

_____

_____

_____

Reason for visit _____

Date _____   Doctor _____

Describe problem, if any _____

Cause of problem _____

Doctor's advice and treatment _____

_____

_____

Tests performed, if any _____

Test results _____

Recommended follow-up _____

_____

Questions to ask during this visit _____

_____

_____

_____

_____

_____

Doctor's answers and comments _____

_____

_____

_____

_____

_____

Diary of Doctors' Appointments

Reason for visit _____

Date _____   Doctor _____

Describe problem, if any _____

Cause of problem _____

Doctor's advice and treatment _____

_____

_____

Tests performed, if any _____

Test results _____

Recommended follow-up _____

_____

Questions to ask during this visit _____

_____

_____

_____

_____

_____

_____

Doctor's answers and comments _____

_____

_____

_____

_____

_____

Reason for visit _____

Date _____   Doctor _____

Describe problem, if any _____

Cause of problem _____

Doctor's advice and treatment _____

_____

_____

Tests performed, if any _____

Test results _____

Recommended follow-up _____

_____

Questions to ask during this visit _____

_____

_____

_____

_____

_____

Doctor's answers and comments _____

_____

_____

_____

_____

Diary of Doctors' Appointments

Diary of Doctors' Appointments

Reason for visit _____

Date _____   Doctor _____

Describe problem, if any _____

Cause of problem _____

Doctor's advice and treatment _____

_____

_____

Tests performed, if any _____

Test results _____

Recommended follow-up _____

_____

Questions to ask during this visit _____

_____

_____

_____

_____

_____

Doctor's answers and comments _____

_____

_____

_____

_____

Reason for visit _____

Date _____   Doctor _____

Describe problem, if any _____

Cause of problem _____

Doctor's advice and treatment _____

_____

_____

Tests performed, if any _____

Test results _____

Recommended follow-up _____

_____

Questions to ask during this visit _____

_____

_____

_____

_____

_____

Doctor's answers and comments _____

_____

_____

_____

_____

_____

**Diary of
Doctors'
Appointments**

43

Diary of Doctors' Appointments

Reason for visit _____

Date _____   Doctor _____

Describe problem, if any _____

Cause of problem _____

Doctor's advice and treatment _____

_____

_____

Tests performed, if any _____

Test results _____

Recommended follow-up _____

_____

Questions to ask during this visit _____

_____

_____

_____

_____

_____

_____

Doctor's answers and comments _____

_____

_____

_____

_____

_____

Reason for visit _____

Date _____   Doctor _____

Describe problem, if any _____

Cause of problem _____

Doctor's advice and treatment _____

_____

_____

Tests performed, if any _____

Test results _____

Recommended follow-up _____

_____

Questions to ask during this visit _____

_____

_____

_____

_____

_____

Doctor's answers and comments _____

_____

_____

_____

_____

_____

Diary of Doctors' Appointments

Reason for visit _____

Date _____   Doctor _____

Describe problem, if any _____

Cause of problem _____

Doctor's advice and treatment _____

_____

_____

Tests performed, if any _____

Test results _____

Recommended follow-up _____

_____

Questions to ask during this visit _____

_____

_____

_____

_____

_____

_____

Doctor's answers and comments _____

_____

_____

_____

_____

_____

_____

Reason for visit _____

Date _____   Doctor _____

Describe problem, if any _____

Cause of problem _____

Doctor's advice and treatment _____

_____

_____

Tests performed, if any _____

Test results _____

Recommended follow-up _____

_____

Questions to ask during this visit _____

_____

_____

_____

_____

_____

Doctor's answers and comments _____

_____

_____

_____

_____

_____

Diary of Doctors' Appointments

Reason for visit _____

Date _____   Doctor _____

Describe problem, if any _____

Cause of problem _____

Doctor's advice and treatment _____

_____

_____

Tests performed, if any _____

Test results _____

Recommended follow-up _____

_____

Questions to ask during this visit _____

_____

_____

_____

_____

_____

Doctor's answers and comments _____

_____

_____

_____

_____

_____

Reason for visit _____

Date _____   Doctor _____

Describe problem, if any _____

Cause of problem _____

Doctor's advice and treatment _____

_____

_____

Tests performed, if any _____

Test results _____

Recommended follow-up _____

_____

Questions to ask during this visit _____

_____

_____

_____

_____

_____

_____

Doctor's answers and comments _____

_____

_____

_____

_____

**Diary of
Doctors'
Appointments**

Diary of Doctors' Appointments

Reason for visit _____

Date _____   Doctor _____

Describe problem, if any _____

Cause of problem _____

Doctor's advice and treatment _____

_____

_____

Tests performed, if any _____

Test results _____

Recommended follow-up _____

_____

Questions to ask during this visit _____

_____

_____

_____

_____

_____

_____

Doctor's answers and comments _____

_____

_____

_____

_____

_____

Reason for visit _____

Date _____   Doctor _____

Describe problem, if any _____

Cause of problem _____

Doctor's advice and treatment _____

_____

_____

Tests performed, if any _____

Test results _____

Recommended follow-up _____

_____

Questions to ask during this visit _____

_____

_____

_____

_____

_____

_____

Doctor's answers and comments _____

_____

_____

_____

_____

Diary of Doctors' Appointments

Reason for visit _____

Date _____   Doctor _____

Describe problem, if any _____

Cause of problem _____

Doctor's advice and treatment _____

_____

_____

Tests performed, if any _____

Test results _____

Recommended follow-up _____

_____

Questions to ask during this visit _____

_____

_____

_____

_____

_____

_____

Doctor's answers and comments _____

_____

_____

_____

_____

_____

Reason for visit _____

Date _____ Doctor _____

Describe problem, if any _____

Cause of problem _____

Doctor's advice and treatment _____

_____

_____

Tests performed, if any _____

Test results _____

Recommended follow-up _____

_____

Questions to ask during this visit _____

_____

_____

_____

_____

_____

Doctor's answers and comments _____

_____

_____

_____

_____

_____

Diary of Doctors' Appointments

Reason for visit _____

Date _____   Doctor _____

Describe problem, if any _____

Cause of problem _____

Doctor's advice and treatment _____

_____

_____

Tests performed, if any _____

Test results _____

Recommended follow-up _____

_____

Questions to ask during this visit _____

_____

_____

_____

_____

_____

Doctor's answers and comments _____

_____

_____

_____

_____

_____

Reason for visit —————————————————————————

Date —————————— Doctor ————————————————

Describe problem, if any ————————————————————

Cause of problem ———————————————————————

Doctor's advice and treatment ————————————————

——————————————————————————————————

——————————————————————————————————

Tests performed, if any ——————————————————————

Test results ——————————————————————————

Recommended follow-up ——————————————————————

——————————————————————————————————

Questions to ask during this visit ————————————————

——————————————————————————————————

——————————————————————————————————

——————————————————————————————————

——————————————————————————————————

——————————————————————————————————

——————————————————————————————————

Doctor's answers and comments ————————————————

——————————————————————————————————

——————————————————————————————————

——————————————————————————————————

——————————————————————————————————

——————————————————————————————————

Diary of Doctors' Appointments

Reason for visit _____

Date _____   Doctor _____

Describe problem, if any _____

Cause of problem _____

Doctor's advice and treatment _____

_____

_____

Tests performed, if any _____

Test results _____

Recommended follow-up _____

_____

Questions to ask during this visit _____

_____

_____

_____

_____

_____

_____

Doctor's answers and comments _____

_____

_____

_____

_____

_____

Reason for visit _____

Date _____   Doctor _____

Describe problem, if any _____

Cause of problem _____

Doctor's advice and treatment _____

_____

_____

Tests performed, if any _____

Test results _____

Recommended follow-up _____

_____

Questions to ask during this visit _____

_____

_____

_____

_____

_____

Doctor's answers and comments _____

_____

_____

_____

_____

Diary of Doctors' Appointments

Reason for visit _____

Date _____   Doctor _____

Describe problem, if any _____

Cause of problem _____

Doctor's advice and treatment _____

_____

_____

Tests performed, if any _____

Test results _____

Recommended follow-up _____

_____

Questions to ask during this visit _____

_____

_____

_____

_____

_____

_____

Doctor's answers and comments _____

_____

_____

_____

_____

_____

Reason for visit _____

Date _____ Doctor _____

Describe problem, if any _____

Cause of problem _____

Doctor's advice and treatment _____

_____

_____

Tests performed, if any _____

Test results _____

Recommended follow-up _____

_____

Questions to ask during this visit _____

_____

_____

_____

_____

_____

Doctor's answers and comments _____

_____

_____

_____

_____

_____

**Diary of
Doctors'
Appointments**

59

Diary of Doctors' Appointments

Reason for visit _____

Date _____   Doctor _____

Describe problem, if any _____

Cause of problem _____

Doctor's advice and treatment _____

_____

_____

Tests performed, if any _____

Test results _____

Recommended follow-up _____

_____

Questions to ask during this visit _____

_____

_____

_____

_____

_____

Doctor's answers and comments _____

_____

_____

_____

_____

_____

Reason for visit _____

Date _____ Doctor _____

Describe problem, if any _____

Cause of problem _____

Doctor's advice and treatment _____

_____

_____

Tests performed, if any _____

Test results _____

Recommended follow-up _____

_____

Questions to ask during this visit _____

_____

_____

_____

_____

_____

Doctor's answers and comments _____

_____

_____

_____

_____

Diary of Doctors' Appointments

Reason for visit _____

Date _____   Doctor _____

Describe problem, if any _____

Cause of problem _____

Doctor's advice and treatment _____

_____

_____

Tests performed, if any _____

Test results _____

Recommended follow-up _____

_____

Questions to ask during this visit _____

_____

_____

_____

_____

_____

_____

Doctor's answers and comments _____

_____

_____

_____

_____

_____

Reason for visit _____

Date _____   Doctor _____

Describe problem, if any _____

Cause of problem _____

Doctor's advice and treatment _____

_____

_____

Tests performed, if any _____

Test results _____

Recommended follow-up _____

_____

Questions to ask during this visit _____

_____

_____

_____

_____

_____

Doctor's answers and comments _____

_____

_____

_____

_____

Diary of Doctors' Appointments

Reason for visit _____

Date _____   Doctor _____

Describe problem, if any _____

Cause of problem _____

Doctor's advice and treatment _____

_____

_____

Tests performed, if any _____

Test results _____

Recommended follow-up _____

_____

Questions to ask during this visit _____

_____

_____

_____

_____

_____

Doctor's answers and comments _____

_____

_____

_____

_____

Reason for visit _____

Date _____   Doctor _____

Describe problem, if any _____

Cause of problem _____

Doctor's advice and treatment _____

_____

_____

Tests performed, if any _____

Test results _____

Recommended follow-up _____

_____

Questions to ask during this visit _____

_____

_____

_____

_____

_____

Doctor's answers and comments _____

_____

_____

_____

_____

_____

Diary of Doctors' Appointments

Reason for visit _____

Date _____   Doctor _____

Describe problem, if any _____

Cause of problem _____

Doctor's advice and treatment _____

_____

_____

Tests performed, if any _____

Test results _____

Recommended follow-up _____

_____

Questions to ask during this visit _____

_____

_____

_____

_____

_____

Doctor's answers and comments _____

_____

_____

_____

_____

_____

Reason for visit _____

Date _____   Doctor _____

Describe problem, if any _____

Cause of problem _____

Doctor's advice and treatment _____

_____

_____

Tests performed, if any _____

Test results _____

Recommended follow-up _____

_____

Questions to ask during this visit _____

_____

_____

_____

_____

_____

Doctor's answers and comments _____

_____

_____

_____

_____

**Diary of
Doctors'
Appointments**

Diary of Doctors' Appointments

Reason for visit _____

Date _____   Doctor _____

Describe problem, if any _____

Cause of problem _____

Doctor's advice and treatment _____

_____

_____

Tests performed, if any _____

Test results _____

Recommended follow-up _____

_____

Questions to ask during this visit _____

_____

_____

_____

_____

_____

Doctor's answers and comments _____

_____

_____

_____

_____

_____

Reason for visit _____

Date _____   Doctor _____

Describe problem, if any _____

Cause of problem _____

Doctor's advice and treatment _____

_____

_____

Tests performed, if any _____

Test results _____

Recommended follow-up _____

_____

Questions to ask during this visit _____

_____

_____

_____

_____

_____

Doctor's answers and comments _____

_____

_____

_____

_____

_____

**Diary of
Doctors'
Appointments**

Diary of Doctors' Appointments

Reason for visit _____

Date _____   Doctor _____

Describe problem, if any _____

Cause of problem _____

Doctor's advice and treatment _____

_____

_____

Tests performed, if any _____

Test results _____

Recommended follow-up _____

_____

Questions to ask during this visit _____

_____

_____

_____

_____

_____

_____

Doctor's answers and comments _____

_____

_____

_____

_____

_____

Reason for visit _____

Date _____ Doctor _____

Describe problem, if any _____

Cause of problem _____

Doctor's advice and treatment _____

_____

_____

Tests performed, if any _____

Test results _____

Recommended follow-up _____

_____

Questions to ask during this visit _____

_____

_____

_____

_____

_____

Doctor's answers and comments _____

_____

_____

_____

_____

**Diary of
Doctors'
Appointments**

71

**Diary of
Doctors'
Appointments**

Reason for visit _____

Date _____   Doctor _____

Describe problem, if any _____

Cause of problem _____

Doctor's advice and treatment _____

_____

_____

Tests performed, if any _____

Test results _____

Recommended follow-up _____

_____

Questions to ask during this visit _____

_____

_____

_____

_____

_____

_____

Doctor's answers and comments _____

_____

_____

_____

_____

_____

Reason for visit _____

Date _____   Doctor _____

Describe problem, if any _____

Cause of problem _____

Doctor's advice and treatment _____

_____

_____

Tests performed, if any _____

Test results _____

Recommended follow-up _____

_____

Questions to ask during this visit _____

_____

_____

_____

_____

_____

_____

Doctor's answers and comments _____

_____

_____

_____

_____

_____

Diary of Doctors' Appointments

Reason for visit _____

Date _____ Doctor _____

Describe problem, if any _____

Cause of problem _____

Doctor's advice and treatment _____

_____

_____

Tests performed, if any _____

Test results _____

Recommended follow-up _____

_____

Questions to ask during this visit _____

_____

_____

_____

_____

_____

_____

Doctor's answers and comments _____

_____

_____

_____

_____

_____

MEDICAL AND HEALTH SCREENING TESTS

There's no ironclad schedule for most tests. Which ones you need (and how often) depends on your age, risk factors and sense of vigilance, as well as your doctor's approach to preventive medicine.

The American Cancer Society's recommendations for cancer testing are included here, though your doctor may alter the schedule. Other procedures are listed, too. Try showing her this section, and asking her to suggest a timetable. (Write it in pencil; it may change over time.)

Finally, record all tests you take and their results on the worksheets that follow.

MY BLOOD PRESSURE AND CHOLESTEROL READINGS

Date	Blood pressure	Triglycer-ides	Choles-terol	HDL (high-density lipopro-teins)	Ratio: choles-terol di-vided by HDL ʰᴰᴸ	Medication prescribed, if any
July 2001		1.38	5.48	1.35	3.5	

My Doctor's Advice on Lowering Blood Pressure or Cholesterol

normal cholesterol 5.4

LDL should be less than 3.4

Cancer Test Guidelines

THE AMERICAN CANCER SOCIETY'S
TEST RECOMMENDATIONS

Test or procedure	Gender	Age	How often	My doctor's recommendation
Sigmoidoscopy	M & F	50 and over	Every 3 to 5 years, based on doctor's advice	
Stool guaiac slide test	M & F	Over 50	Every year	
Digital rectal examination	M & F	Over 40	Every year	
PSA blood test for prostate cancer	M	50 and over	Every year	
Pap test	F	Starting at sexual activity or age 18	Every year (may become less frequent based on results and doctor's advice)	

Test or procedure	Gender	Age	How often	My doctor's recommendation
Pelvic exam	F	18 to 40	Every 1 to 3 years with Pap test	
		Over 40	Every year	
Endometrial tissue sample	F	At menopause, women at high risk*	At menopause, then at doctor's discretion	
Breast self-exam	F	20 and older	Every month	
Mammogram†	F	40 to 49	Every 1 to 2 years	
		50 and over	Every year	
Cancer checkup (a physical exam)‡	M & F	Over 20	Every 3 years	
		Over 40	Every year	

*History of infertility, obesity, failure to ovulate, abnormal uterine bleeding, or estrogen therapy.
†Screening mammography should begin by age 40.
‡To include examination for cancers of the thyroid, testicles, prostate, ovaries, lymph nodes, oral region, and skin.

RECORD OF X RAYS

Date	Type of X ray	Result	Doctor who read the X ray	Doctor who has X ray on file

MY MEDICAL TEST RESULTS

Add your own notes on what the results signify, your doctor's interpretation, recommended follow-up, and treatment options.

Test	Date	Results	Notes

Medical and Health Screening Tests

Test	Date	Results	Notes

Test	Date	Results	Notes

Medical and Health Screening Tests

**Medical and
Health
Screening Tests**

Test	Date	Results	Notes

PAST HOSPITALIZATIONS AND SURGERIES

Try to go back to childhood with this section. If you can't recall details, just note the procedure and roughly when it happened. (A call to the doctor or hospital might produce more information.) Include same-day surgeries, even if they were done in a doctor's office.

Your hospital records are filed under a patient record number. It's not essential, but if a doctor ever needs your file fast, having this number can speed up the process. You can get it by calling or writing to the hospital.

Use the separate Hospitalization Diary on page 88 to track any future hospitalization.

HISTORY OF HOSPITALIZATIONS

Date or year	Problem	Type of surgery or treatment	Doctor or sur-geon	Hospital	Patient record number	Results and other notes

Date or year	Problem	Type of surgery or treatment	Doctor or surgeon	Hospital	Patient record number	Results and other notes

Hospitalization diary

These worksheets cover tests, medications, and day-by-day notes on your stay. Use the margins if you have to, and write down anything that seems important—it may be useful later. If you're in the hospital longer than six days or more than once, copy the format into a notebook.

Reason for hospitalization _____

Hospital (address and telephone) _____

_____

Date admitted _____ Date discharged_____

Room no. _____Telephone no. _____ Patient record no. _____

Primary doctor _____

Primary surgeon _____

Names of other doctors seen _____

_____

_____

Names of nurses, other staffers I want to remember _____

_____

RECORD OF TESTS AND PROCEDURES

Date	Name of test or procedure	Who performed it	Why performed	Results or doctor's interpretation	Side effects, if any

RECORD OF MEDICATIONS

Date/ time	Drug	Dosage	Reason for medi- cation	Results	Side effects, if any

Journal entries

■ **DAY 1** ■

_____
Date

Doctor(s) seen today _____

What was discussed _____

What was decided _____

Overall, how did you feel today? _____
_____

Notes on diet _____

Notes on discomfort or pain _____

Questions to ask the doctor _____
_____
_____
_____
_____
_____

Notes and details on tests, procedures, medications _____
_____
_____
_____
_____
_____
_____
_____

■ **DAY 2** ■

_____

Date

Doctor(s) seen today _____

What was discussed _____

What was decided _____

Overall, how did you feel today? _____

_____

Notes on diet _____

Notes on discomfort or pain _____

Questions to ask the doctor _____

_____

_____

_____

_____

_____

Notes and details on tests, procedures, medications _____

_____

_____

_____

_____

_____

_____

_____

_____

■ DAY 3 ■

_____

Date

Doctor(s) seen today _____

What was discussed _____

What was decided _____

Overall, how did you feel today? _____

_____

Notes on diet _____

Notes on discomfort or pain _____

Questions to ask the doctor _____

_____

_____

_____

_____

_____

Notes and details on tests, procedures, medications _____

_____

_____

_____

_____

_____

_____

_____

■ **DAY 4** ■

_____

Date

Doctor(s) seen today _____

What was discussed _____

What was decided _____

Overall, how did you feel today? _____

_____

Notes on diet _____

Notes on discomfort or pain _____

Questions to ask the doctor _____

_____

_____

_____

_____

_____

Notes and details on tests, procedures, medications _____

_____

_____

_____

_____

_____

_____

_____

■ DAY 5 ■

_____

Date

Doctor(s) seen today _____

What was discussed _____

What was decided _____

Overall, how did you feel today? _____

_____

Notes on diet _____

Notes on discomfort or pain _____

Questions to ask the doctor _____

_____

_____

_____

_____

_____

Notes and details on tests, procedures, medications _____

_____

_____

_____

_____

_____

_____

_____

■ DAY 6 ■

Date

Doctor(s) seen today _____

What was discussed _____

What was decided _____

Overall, how did you feel today? _____

_____

Notes on diet _____

Notes on discomfort or pain _____

Questions to ask the doctor _____

_____

_____

_____

_____

_____

Notes and details on tests, procedures, medications _____

_____

_____

_____

_____

_____

_____

_____

FOR WOMEN ONLY

These worksheets can help organize a very specialized aspect of your medical history.

If you are keeping tabs on a long-term condition, like fertility problems or a pregnancy, the Record of Special Conditions offers room for more notes.

A Woman's Medical History

Age when menstruation began _____

Describe any irregularities or problems with your menstrual cycle. _____

_____

_____

_____

_____

Have you ever had surgery (including biopsy) on your breasts or reproductive system? Give details and dates. _____

_____

_____

_____

_____

Do you take female hormones? Name the medication, dosage, when it was
first prescribed, and why. _____

_____

Have you ever had a sexually transmitted disease? Name the condition, the
year, and the treatment. _____

_____

_____

Birth control method used now, if any _____

_____

Birth control methods used in the past _____

_____

Describe any side effects or complications related to birth control. _____

_____

_____

PREGNANCY AND CHILDBIRTH

Note the details of any pregnancies below.

	Date of baby's birth (or year of pregnancy)	Vaginal or C-section?	If pregnancy ended in abortion, stillbirth, or miscarriage, describe	Complications or other notes
Pregnancy no. 1				
no. 2				
no. 3				

If you have ever had difficulty getting pregnant, give details. _____

_____

_____

_____

Are you trying to get pregnant now? Give details. _____

_____

_____

FIVE-YEAR MENSTRUATION CALENDAR

Doctors often need to know when a patient had her last period, but it's hard to recall without writing it down. Starting with the current year, enter the dates down one column at a time. *Remember to do a breast check after each period ends.*

	19 ____	19 ____	19 ____	19 ____	19 ____
January					
February					
March					
April					
May					
June					
July					
August					
September					
October					
November					
December					

PAP TEST RESULTS

If you want to keep all your gynecological records in one place, track Pap test results here, instead of in the chapter on medical tests. Pap results are described as Class I, II, III, IV, or V, but gynecologists often add a verbal description. Ask if there are details you can add to this worksheet.

Date	Results/Class	Details

BREAST CHECKS

Check your own breasts monthly, just after your period; your physician can show you the technique. If anything out of the ordinary is revealed by your self-exam, a physical, or mammogram, start taking notes immediately. Use these pages to keep track of tests, procedures, results, and medical advice.

Date	Observations

Date	Observations	For Women Only
_____	_____	
_____	_____	
_____	_____	
_____	_____	
_____	_____	
_____	_____	
_____	_____	
_____	_____	
_____	_____	
_____	_____	
_____	_____	
_____	_____	
_____	_____	
_____	_____	
_____	_____	
_____	_____	
_____	_____	
_____	_____	
_____	_____	
_____	_____	
_____	_____	
_____	_____	
_____	_____	
_____	_____	
_____	_____	

103

For Women Only

Date	Observations
_____	_____
_____	_____
_____	_____
_____	_____
_____	_____
_____	_____
_____	_____
_____	_____
_____	_____
_____	_____
_____	_____
_____	_____
_____	_____
_____	_____
_____	_____
_____	_____
_____	_____
_____	_____
_____	_____
_____	_____
_____	_____
_____	_____
_____	_____
_____	_____
_____	_____
_____	_____
_____	_____
_____	_____

Headache Journal

Millions of people suffer from regular headaches. If over-the-counter pain-killers don't banish yours, try keeping a record of the pain. Only with this kind of precise description can a doctor diagnose the headaches (there are several kinds) and decide what medication or treatment is best.

Headache Journal

Date and hour headache began	Severity: mild 1 moderate 2 intense 3 severe 4	Location of headache (e.g., across forehead, behind left eye, etc.)	Other symptoms (e.g., dizziness, nausea, fatigue, loss of balance, light sensitivity)

How long did the headache last?	Any stressful events or situations that preceded the headache?	Medications you took for this headache	Relief: none 0 mild 1 moderate 2 complete 3	Notes about mood, sleep, appetite, worries, and emotional state

Headache Journal

Headache Journal

Date and hour headache began	Severity: mild 1 moderate 2 intense 3 severe 4	Location of headache (e.g., across forehead, behind left eye, etc.)	Other symptoms (e.g., dizziness, nausea, fatigue, loss of balance, light sensitivity)

How long did the headache last?	Any stressful events or situations that preceded the headache?	Medications you took for this headache	Relief: none 0 mild 1 moderate 2 complete 3	Notes about mood, sleep, appetite, worries, and emotional state

Headache Journal

Headache Journal

Date and hour headache began	Severity: mild 1 moderate 2 intense 3 severe 4	Location of headache (e.g., across forehead, behind left eye, etc.)	Other symptoms (e.g., dizziness, nausea, fatigue, loss of balance, light sensitivity)

How long did the headache last?	Any stressful events or situations that preceded the headache?	Medications you took for this headache	Relief: none 0 mild 1 moderate 2 complete 3	Notes about mood, sleep, appetite, worries, and emotional state

Headache Journal

Headache Journal

Date and hour headache began	Severity: mild 1 moderate 2 intense 3 severe 4	Location of headache (e.g., across forehead, behind left eye, etc.)	Other symptoms (e.g., dizziness, nausea, fatigue, loss of balance, light sensitivity)

How long did the headache last?	Any stressful events or situations that preceded the headache?	Medications you took for this headache	Relief: none 0 mild 1 moderate 2 complete 3	Notes about mood, sleep, appetite, worries, and emotional state

Headache Journal

RECORD OF SPECIAL CONDITIONS

If you're following or treating a long-term condition, you may want extra space for notes. These pages are intentionally blank so you can structure your records as you wish. (You may want to borrow a format that's proved useful to you in another chapter.) Tip: Start each entry with the date, and end it with any questions you want to remember to ask.

_____

_____

_____

_____

_____

_____

_____

_____

_____

_____

**Record of
Special
Conditions**

**Record of
Special
Conditions**

WEIGHT, DIET, AND EXERCISE LOG

If you are watching your weight, keeping a worksheet might be helpful. Weekly entries can give you a better picture, over time, than daily ones.

Date	Weight	Dieting notes	Exercise notes

Date	Weight	Dieting notes	Exercise notes

Weight, Diet, and Excercise Log

Weight, Diet, and Excercise Log

Date	Weight	Dieting notes	Exercise notes

Date	Weight	Dieting notes	Exercise notes

Weight, Diet, and Excercise Log

MEDICAL BILLS AND PAYMENTS

This worksheet can help track bills you've paid, reimbursements you're owed, and, in the last column, amounts not covered by insurance. (You may be able to deduct this from taxable income.)

Use separate lines for lab tests and for submissions to a secondary insurance company or health care spending account.

Date of visit	Name of doctor or provider	Amount of bill	Date & amount I paid

Date I sent bill to insurance co.	Date of reimbursement	Amount covered by insurance	Check sent to me or doctor?	Amount not covered

Medical Bills and Payments

Medical Bills and Payments

Date of visit	Name of doctor or provider	Amount of bill	Date & amount I paid

Date I sent bill to insurance co.	Date of reimbursement	Amount covered by insurance	Check sent to me or doctor?	Amount not covered

Medical Bills and Payments

Medical Bills and Payments

Date of visit	Name of doctor or provider	Amount of bill	Date & amount I paid

Date I sent bill to insurance co.	Date of reimbursement	Amount covered by insurance	Check sent to me or doctor?	Amount not covered

Medical Bills and Payments

A CHILD'S DIARY OF HEALTH

If you are keeping this workbook for a child, start here. Use the next chapter as a journal of visits to the pediatrician, then fill in the rest of the book as you would for yourself.

Feel free to ask your obstetrician and pediatrician to check their notes if you can't fill in all the key details.

Background

Child's name _____

Child's date of birth _____

Social Security number _____

Obstetrician (name, address, telephone) _____

_____

Hospital where born (name, address, telephone) _____

_____

Child's patient record number _____

Pediatrician seen in hospital (name, address, telephone) _____

_____

Medical Data

Blood type _____

Allergies _____

Medical problems _____

Required medications _____

Pregnancy and Birth History

Date of birth _____ Time of birth _____

Weight at birth _____

Height at birth _____

Head circumference at birth _____

Did baby arrive early or late? Describe _____

Type of birth: Vaginal _____ C-section _____

Forceps used? Details _____

PKU test results: positive ☐ negative ☐ Apgar score _____
   (The Apgar score is a rating of your baby's condition at birth. Up to 2 points each are given for baby's color, muscle tone, heart rate, respiratory rate, and response to stimulus.)

   If positive, describe details and follow-up _____

_____

Feeding: Breast ____ Bottle ____ Type of formula _____

Describe any problems or treatments during pregnancy _____

_____

_____

Describe any problems or treatments during or after birth _____

_____

_____

Drugs taken by mother during pregnancy _____

Drugs taken during childbirth _____

Drugs taken during breast-feeding _____

Note any workplace or environmental hazards that could have affected either parent at time of conception, or mother during pregnancy _____

_____

If Baby Was Adopted

Date and place of adoption _____

Agency or lawyer involved (name, address, telephone) _____

_____

Place of birth (including hospital, if known) _____

_____

Birth parents, if known (name, address, telephone) _____

_____

Describe anything known about medical and genetic history of baby and birth parents _____

_____

_____

(If possible, ask birth mother to fill out the Family column of the medical history section.)

Notes on Child's Health and Habits

Use this page for any details on your child's health, including sleeping or feeding habits.

_____

_____

_____

_____

_____

_____

_____

_____

_____

_____

_____

_____

_____

_____

_____

_____

_____

_____

_____

_____

_____

_____

_____

_____

CHILD'S DIARY OF PEDIATRIC VISITS

You'll probably see a lot of the pediatrician, both for well-baby visits and an assortment of colds, ear infections and other minor illnesses. These pages are your record of vaccinations, tests, growth, and, in the page-by-page diary, doctors' visits. If questions crop up, write them down *before* the appointment.

When the section is full, switch over to the Diary of Doctors' Appointments for adults.

Well-Baby Checkups

The American Academy of Pediatrics suggests checkups for your baby at the ages listed. Your pediatrician may change the times to suit your child. After age 6, the Academy recommends visits every two years until age 20.

Recommended age	Date of visit
Newborn	_____
2 to 4 weeks	_____
2 months	_____
4 months	_____

Recommended age	Date of visit
6 months	_____
9 months	_____
12 months	_____
15 months	_____
18 months	_____
2 years	_____
3 years	_____
4 years	_____
5 years	_____
6 years	_____

Child's Diary of Pediatric Visits

Vaccination Log and Worksheet

This schedule is recommended by the American Academy of Pediatrics though your doctor may vary the timetable slightly:

Age	Vaccination	Date given
Birth	Hepatitis B vaccine	_____
1 to 2 mos.	Hepatitis B vaccine	_____
2 months	DTP, polio, Hib	_____
4 months	DTP, polio, Hib	_____
6 months	DTP, Hib	_____
6 to 18 mos.	Hepatitis B vaccine, polio	_____
12 to 15 months	Hib, MMR	_____
15 to 18 months	DTP	_____
4 to 6 years	DTP, polio	_____
11 to 12 years	MMR	_____
14 to 16 years	Tetanus-Diphtheria	_____

Child's Diary of Pediatric Visits

Your pediatrician may also set a schedule for the tests below.

Test	Date	Results & notes
Urinalysis	_____	_____
Hematocrit	_____	_____
Lead test	_____	_____
Tine (for TB)	_____	_____
Blood pressure	_____	_____
Anemia	_____	_____
Vision	_____	_____
_____	_____	_____
_____	_____	_____
_____	_____	_____
_____	_____	_____
_____	_____	_____
_____	_____	_____
_____	_____	_____

GROWTH RECORD

When your child is weighed and measured at the doctor's office, keep the results here. (Head circumference is only measured for about 2 years.)

Date & age	Height	Weight	Head size	Date & age	Height	Weight	Head size

Diary of Pediatric Visits

Reason for visit _____

Date _____ Doctor's name _____

Describe problem, if any _____

_____

Doctor's advice and treatment _____

_____

_____

Tests performed, if any, and results _____

_____

Recommended follow-up _____

Questions to ask the pediatrician _____

_____

_____

Child's height _____ and weight_____, if measured.

Reason for visit _____

Date _____ Doctor's name _____

Describe problem, if any _____

_____

Doctor's advice and treatment _____

_____

_____

Tests performed, if any, and results _____

_____

Recommended follow-up _____

Questions to ask the pediatrician _____

_____

_____

Child's height _____ and weight_____, if measured.

Child's Diary of Pediatric Visits

Reason for visit _____

Date _____ Doctor's name _____

Describe problem, if any _____

_____

Doctor's advice and treatment _____

_____

_____

Tests performed, if any, and results _____

_____

Recommended follow-up _____

Questions to ask the pediatrician _____

_____

_____

Child's height _____ and weight_____, if measured.

Reason for visit _____

Date _____ Doctor's name _____

Describe problem, if any _____

_____

Doctor's advice and treatment _____

_____

_____

Tests performed, if any, and results _____

_____

Recommended follow-up _____

Questions to ask the pediatrician _____

_____

_____

Child's height _____ and weight _____, if measured.

Child's Diary of Pediatric Visits

Reason for visit _____

Date _____ Doctor's name _____

Describe problem, if any _____

_____

Doctor's advice and treatment _____

_____

_____

Tests performed, if any, and results _____

_____

Recommended follow-up _____

Questions to ask the pediatrician _____

_____

_____

Child's height _____ and weight_____, if measured.

Reason for visit _____

Date _____ Doctor's name _____

Describe problem, if any _____

_____

Doctor's advice and treatment _____

_____

_____

Tests performed, if any, and results _____

_____

Recommended follow-up _____

Questions to ask the pediatrician _____

_____

_____

Child's height _____ and weight _____, if measured.

Child's Diary of Pediatric Visits

Reason for visit _____

Date _____ Doctor's name _____

Describe problem, if any _____

_____

Doctor's advice and treatment _____

_____

_____

Tests performed, if any, and results _____

_____

Recommended follow-up _____

Questions to ask the pediatrician _____

_____

_____

Child's height _____ and weight_____, if measured.

Reason for visit _____

Date _____ Doctor's name _____

Describe problem, if any _____

_____

Doctor's advice and treatment _____

_____

_____

Tests performed, if any, and results _____

_____

Recommended follow-up _____

Questions to ask the pediatrician _____

_____

_____

Child's height _____ and weight _____, if measured.

Child's Diary of
Pediatric Visits

Reason for visit _____

Date _____ Doctor's name _____

Describe problem, if any _____

_____

Doctor's advice and treatment _____

_____

_____

Tests performed, if any, and results _____

_____

Recommended follow-up _____

Questions to ask the pediatrician _____

_____

_____

Child's height _____ and weight_____, if measured.

Reason for visit _____

Date _____ Doctor's name _____

Describe problem, if any _____

_____

Doctor's advice and treatment _____

_____

_____

Tests performed, if any, and results _____

_____

Recommended follow-up _____

Questions to ask the pediatrician _____

_____

_____

Child's height _____ and weight_____, if measured.

Child's Diary of Pediatric Visits

Reason for visit _____

Date _____ Doctor's name _____

Describe problem, if any _____

_____

Doctor's advice and treatment _____

_____

_____

Tests performed, if any, and results _____

_____

Recommended follow-up _____

Questions to ask the pediatrician _____

_____

_____

Child's height _____ and weight_____, if measured.

Reason for visit _____

Date _____ Doctor's name _____

Describe problem, if any _____

_____

Doctor's advice and treatment _____

_____

_____

Tests performed, if any, and results _____

_____

Recommended follow-up _____

Questions to ask the pediatrician _____

_____

_____

Child's height _____ and weight_____, if measured.

Reason for visit _____

Date _____ Doctor's name _____

Describe problem, if any _____

_____

Doctor's advice and treatment _____

_____

_____

Tests performed, if any, and results _____

_____

Recommended follow-up _____

Questions to ask the pediatrician _____

_____

_____

Child's height _____ and weight _____, if measured.

Reason for visit _____

Date _____ Doctor's name _____

Describe problem, if any _____

_____

Doctor's advice and treatment _____

_____

_____

Tests performed, if any, and results _____

_____

Recommended follow-up _____

Questions to ask the pediatrician _____

_____

_____

Child's height _____ and weight_____, if measured.

Child's Diary of Pediatric Visits

Reason for visit _____

Date _____ Doctor's name _____

Describe problem, if any _____

_____

Doctor's advice and treatment _____

_____

_____

Tests performed, if any, and results _____

_____

Recommended follow-up _____

Questions to ask the pediatrician _____

_____

_____

Child's height _____ and weight_____, if measured.

Reason for visit _____

Date _____ Doctor's name _____

Describe problem, if any _____

_____

Doctor's advice and treatment _____

_____

_____

Tests performed, if any, and results _____

_____

Recommended follow-up _____

Questions to ask the pediatrician _____

_____

_____

Child's height _____ and weight_____, if measured.

Child's Diary of Pediatric Visits

Reason for visit _____

Date _____ Doctor's name _____

Describe problem, if any _____

_____

Doctor's advice and treatment _____

_____

_____

Tests performed, if any, and results _____

_____

Recommended follow-up _____

Questions to ask the pediatrician _____

_____

_____

Child's height _____ and weight_____, if measured.

Reason for visit _____

Date _____ Doctor's name _____

Describe problem, if any _____

_____

Doctor's advice and treatment _____

_____

_____

Tests performed, if any, and results _____

_____

Recommended follow-up _____

Questions to ask the pediatrician _____

_____

_____

Child's height _____ and weight_____, if measured.

155

Child's Diary of Pediatric Visits

Reason for visit _____

Date _____ Doctor's name _____

Describe problem, if any _____

_____

Doctor's advice and treatment _____

_____

_____

Tests performed, if any, and results _____

_____

Recommended follow-up _____

Questions to ask the pediatrician _____

_____

_____

Child's height _____ and weight_____, if measured.

Reason for visit _____

Date _____ Doctor's name _____

Describe problem, if any _____

_____

Doctor's advice and treatment _____

_____

_____

Tests performed, if any, and results _____

_____

Recommended follow-up _____

Questions to ask the pediatrician _____

_____

_____

Child's height _____ and weight_____, if measured.

Child's Diary of Pediatric Visits

Reason for visit _____

Date _____ Doctor's name _____

Describe problem, if any _____

_____

Doctor's advice and treatment _____

_____

_____

Tests performed, if any, and results _____

_____

Recommended follow-up _____

Questions to ask the pediatrician _____

_____

_____

Child's height _____ and weight_____, if measured.

Reason for visit _____

Date _____ Doctor's name _____

Describe problem, if any _____

_____

Doctor's advice and treatment _____

_____

_____

Tests performed, if any, and results _____

_____

Recommended follow-up _____

Questions to ask the pediatrician _____

_____

_____

Child's height _____ and weight_____, if measured.

Child's Diary of Pediatric Visits

Reason for visit _____

Date _____ Doctor's name _____

Describe problem, if any _____

_____

Doctor's advice and treatment _____

_____

_____

Tests performed, if any, and results _____

_____

Recommended follow-up _____

Questions to ask the pediatrician _____

_____

_____

Child's height _____ and weight_____, if measured.

Reason for visit _____

Date _____ Doctor's name _____

Describe problem, if any _____

_____

Doctor's advice and treatment _____

_____

_____

Tests performed, if any, and results _____

_____

Recommended follow-up _____

Questions to ask the pediatrician _____

_____

_____

Child's height _____ and weight_____, if measured.

Child's Diary of Pediatric Visits

Reason for visit _____

Date _____ Doctor's name _____

Describe problem, if any _____

_____

Doctor's advice and treatment _____

_____

_____

Tests performed, if any, and results _____

_____

Recommended follow-up _____

Questions to ask the pediatrician _____

_____

_____

Child's height _____ and weight_____, if measured.

MEDICAL RECORDS TO CARRY WHEN YOU TRAVEL

Try not to travel with your medical workbook; it would be hard to reconstruct if lost. Consider having an emergency medical worksheet copied onto microfilm the size of a credit card. One company that does this commercially, suppying its own worksheet and charging $15, is:

> AD Medical
> 315 Thorn Hill Lane, Suite 313
> Middletown, Ohio 45042

Note: Hospital staff may have to read the microfilm fast; type or write neatly on the worksheet. Also, it asks an intelligent question you may want to adapt: whether you have pets at home who need care, and who should be contacted. If it applies, you might cross out "pets" and write in "children."

A second option is to carry a passport-sized booklet that includes worksheets for emergency data. You can buy these Health Journal booklets for men, women, and seniors ($4.95 each) and children ($3.95), as well as a record-keeping book for diabetics ($18.50). Add $1.25 apiece for shipping. Contact:

> Informative Amenities Inc.
> P.O. Box 1280
> Santa Monica, California 90406
> (310) 394-6992

ABOUT THE AUTHOR

Dylan Landis is a contributing editor to *Metropolitan Home* and *American HomeStyle* magazines, the book columnist for *Home* magazine, and the author of *Checklist for Your New Baby*, a shopping handbook for new parents. A former newspaper reporter, she covered medicine for the New Orleans *Times-Picayune* and design for the *Chicago Tribune*, and has written for *The New York Times*. Her next book, *Your Healthy Pregnancy Workbook*, will be published later this year.